THE FIRST BIRD:
Songs of the Dark Body in Flight

By
Edward Bruce Bynum

THE FIRST BIRD
SONGS OF THE DARK BODY IN FLIGHT

EDWARD BRUCE BYNUM

Copyright © 2017
Edward Bruce Bynum

All rights reserved including the right of reproduction in whole or in part in any form.

Cover design by Cara Finch
www.cfinchart.com

Printed in the United States of America

ISBN 978-1-945473-37-1

The Brutal Swan Press
PO Box 3121
Amherst, Massachusetts
01004

For Wally Swist, Poet Laureate of the pioneer valley. I hope the First Bird sings to you and that you sing and sing for many many years to come! Given in friendship and admiration for what you have given to so many others.

Dedication

To the human soul…and the journey we are all on.

Edward Bruce Brown
11/12/17

By the same author

Poetry:

- *The Dreaming Skull*
- *GODZILLANANDA: His Life & Visions*
- *Gospel of the Dark Orisha*
- *THE MAGDALENE POEMS: The Love Letters of Jesus the Christ and Mary Magdalene*
- *The Luminous Heretic*
- *TRANSMIGRATION: A Play for Voices*
- *Chronicles of the Pig & Other Delusions* (Winner of the 2010 Naomi Long Madgett Poetry Prize)

Psychology/Psychiatry:

- *The Family Unconscious: An Invisible Bond*
- *The Dreamlife of Families*
- *The Roots of Transcendence*
- *The African Unconscious: Roots of Ancient Mysticism and Modern Psychology*
- *Why Darkness Matters: The Power of Melanin in the Brain*
- *Legacy: Portrait of an Ancestor*
- *Dark Light Consciousness: Melanin, Serpent Power and the Luminous Matrix of Reality*

Table of Contents

Bird's Fall

The First Bird xi
The Two Legends of Bird's Fall 1
Bird's Idyll 3
The First Bird Falls into "Me" and "I" 5
First Bird Hears Voices 6
First Bird Giving Birth 7
First Bird Feels a Presence 8
First Bird Pushes into the Academy 9
Bird Returns to Poetry 10
Bird Talks to God 12
Bird Talking at a Military Funeral 13
Bird at a Lynching 15
Bird Commits Haiku Fifteen Times 16
Bird's Knowledge 19
Bird's Blessing 20
Bird's Revelation 23
Bird Finds a Poem at the End of the World 26
The First Bird Hears Them Coming
  in A Little Night Music 28
First Bird in a Slipstream
  following Hermes Trismegestus 30
First Bird in an Open Field 33
Bird Talks to the Rain 34
Bird After the Meal 36
Bird & Colleagues Make a Suicide Assessment 37
The First Bird Searches for Beauty 39
First Bird Convalescing 41
The First Bird Overhears Rumors 42

The First Bird Grows More Suspicious	43
Bird's Dream	44
Bird in Therapy	45
The First Bird Makes a Confession	46
The First Bird Receives a Vision	47
Bird Stares into the Mirror	48
Bird Reading His Entrails	49
Bird Gives Away Parts of His Body	51
Bird's Final Failure on Earth	53
Bird in a Flashback Recalls Himself a Constellation	55
The First Bird in Flight	56

Bird Recalls When His Voice Returned To Him.............57

The First Bird Returns To Flight 71
- Bird's Egg Song 71
- The Way of the World He Saw 74
- His Blood Vessel Song to the Great Attractor 75
- Return to the Blood 79
- The Passageway Up from the Skull 81
- The Ascent 86
- The Hour of the Blood 89
- Bird Comes to the River of Beings 92
- Nameless 96
- The Stone Turns 97
- The Return of Desire 100
- The New Birth 102
- Return to the Body 105

Acknowledgements:

"The First Bird," The AUROREAN and Best Indie Lit New England, *"First Bird Hears Voices," "The First Bird Overhears Rumors", "The First Bird Searches for Beauty,"* Silkworm, *"First Bird Feels a Presence,"* Common Ground Review.

Prologue: The First Bird

*Out of his marriage with the sky
The first bird pulled courage,
Then a bottomless barrel of apples,
Then a crimson bosom full of flowers and rusted nails.
Peering under his eyelids he saw the stars, reversed,
Staring back at him
From his other identity,
Like he was under the hood of some driverless car,
Out of control, heading for the wreck.
He arrived on earth
And all the creatures bowed to him
With nothing else left to be said.*

The Two Legends of Bird's Fall

i

When the space between the spaces opened out
A crow, a radiant crow, released
From its black wings
With their bags and implants
A surge of birds screeching across the world,
Leaving black stumps, piles of bones,
Husks from beautiful discarded bodies.
From winding trees, from cast off femurs of the dead,
He pulled himself out of a cataract
At the center of the Milky Way.
From eyelids beyond his seeing,
From the dark code of the newly dead,
From the hook
In his vision, his discolored thigh,
He brought the others.
They took up residence in the stones.
They sought solitude and distance
In the ice below the mountains.
They mixed blood with clear alcohol.
They roiled with a blue fire
In the gutter-hole of his belly.
A twist in eternity opened out.
Before he knew it
He saw the interweaving gravity between electricity
And an amoeba.
He became the ambition of trees.
Trees multiplied.
From some he chose sycamores,
Then the shredding skin of hickories.
Farmers stuck their fingers into the earth,
Came up with grubs, ambitious spiders;
Sailors, dreaming repeatedly of dolphins and eels,
Becoming primal repositories

For planetary secrets wide, instinctive,
Not seen for thousands of years.

ii

The first bird
Drunk, darkest and deepest among the wings
Stepped out;
An alluvial sunset swept in from the west.
Drones of bees, bombardiers,
Came from the forests
Sucking air out the ears of the astonished,
The reclusive, those to frightened to scream or raise their heads.
The bravest took to higher paths,
To pine trees holding eagles aloft,
Their eggs in oval womb pits
For the strong, the merciless, branching out
In the future for the kill.
Others drilled holes into canyon floors
Searching the rivers for a vanished age.
The most beautiful, most courageous, most elusive
Swam confidently through the air, moonlit and cool,
Heads held high, lucid as crocodiles, mouths open
Swallowing whole dreams like visions of the wolf-pack,
The solitary lion, desires of the wound up brooding copper-snakes.
Above clouds from which he came
Pillaging in lighting and gold the gods broke out, roamed,
Throwing their weight around
Like violent noise in a drunken saloon, while
In palatial excess and quantum foam
The deathless stars keeled and collided across
The bleak hypotenuse of space.

Bird's Idyll

He had faith in the earth,
Faith she would dream into existence
A species more sentient, more luminous than he.
He had faith in the deeper music
Moving under the surface of every life
Heard through his fingers,
Touched in its drums,
Felt as a peculiar destiny
Working itself out in the rounding of stones,
In attachments, casual losses
Swimming like leaves and illuminated fish
Through the waters, the minutes of a common day.
He had faith when he dreamed
He took under his eyelids
Memory and color from germinal hours,
Met at the gate of other lives
More vast, more tranquil than his own;
That he fell beyond the sleep of the turtle and the rainbow,
Was visited by those beyond death and life.
He took the red imprisoned in rubies,
Made a new blood
That did not dry in the desert
And was known by his kinsmen of earlier tribes.
He knew among blackbirds and eels
There was a ragged secret about the heart of men
Hidden from science,
Harsher than the religions of the desert and skull.
At midnight, when angels soften,
His eyes were filled with semen and gold,
Every song returning to its author,
Every bird reinventing the sensation of flight,
Every father reimagining himself, his heart,
His coiling wisdom reawakened in his son.
So he took his own wing, subject to mosquito bite,
Resin, the rough exterior of an orange,

Calibrated a new path
Past the onion, the smell of new fabrics,
The toil of dying bees in the mysterious air of the poisoned earth.
He walked into the night,
Beyond the cities, quiet, unscripted,
A cat walking over scattered white stones,
Until came to a new beach,
Older than his birth in a previous life,
Luscious and opal,
Darker, sweeter than the juice of the wild blackberry.

The First Bird Falls into "Me" and "I"

In the black garden
He walked, picking at the ground,
Seeking the god of earth
Who shared his song with the worms.
An embryo appeared, its head
Wobbling from side to side, air hissing,
Swallowing the whole of space.
Bird reached deep into his kidneys,
Pulling up the ureters, the bladder,
The urethra and then the surgeon's camera
With its snake eye, its thin steel tongue.
Then he sucked up the buttocks,
The knees, the ankles and the toes;
Turned and swam up to the throat, the nose,
The holes in the cheekbones,
Then the cider-house temples with their smooth skin over the sulci
    of the brain,
The upward coiling evolutionary bulb,
Until he split the garden
Beyond the brain into a hundred billion stars,
Each with its own separate stars, its own locusts.

First Bird Hears Voices

From the rivers came horsemen,
Mud on the hooves,
Night covering their heads in turrets of wind and undertones.
It died down.
From behind windows, without curtains,
A blur of faces opened out with mouths
Moving in slow motion, vowels shaped round like tomatoes
With the red periphery either lipstick or blood.
Then it faded.
On his skin beneath the feathers
Fleas in conversations with each other burrowed deeper
Than his beak could reach,
His quills penetrate.
Inside his ear, canyon of ricochets and echoes,
Bats swam up with their radar songs,
Arias to his first love.
From behind his back
His mother's prophesy drifted in low like smoke,
Filling the valley of his self-esteem
With old cans, bits of rusted out pipes,
Bemused animals exiled from his dreams.
From his genitals came rebellion,
Male and female rioting for dominance,
Riddling the walls with bullet holes,
Parading fetishes intoxicating his memory,
Organs twisting from one sex to another,
Egg and sperm alternating their voices
Beneath the cocoon of feathers.

And the final calamity, the stillborn muse,
Stalking his garden of identity,
Calling out to every object to be "me" and "I",
To embody his name,
Stand and speak out loud to a standing ovation.

First Bird Giving Birth

When his belly swelled beyond the usual borders
He thought the fish he had eaten was bad,
Gas trapped, expanding
At an exponential rate.
When the kicking began
He felt the earth giving up its dead
From the last war, taking no prisoners,
Exotic weapons having been licensed by even the smallest nations.
When the labor began
He felt the continents drifting apart,
Giraffes on one side, reptiles and burrowing beasts
On the other with birds
Flailing about the sky,
Unable to make a lasting decision.
When the blood burst, the water ran,
And the bulb at the base of his spine began to ring,
He thought the second coming of Christ
Had been rescheduled
Centuries earlier than the prophecies had foretold,
The new conqueror arriving
With an army failing the test of forgiveness.
When the vulva opened, the egg popped out,
The swinging doors waving like dark fins in a swamp,
He was horrified at his own creation,
Marveling at the same time on the perfect ellipse of its shape,
The Euclidian dreams it would inspire.
And when the egg hatched, when the perfect inner kingdom
Exploded out, he got to choose
From among fables of the misshapen, children of the snakes,
An owl's skull recovered from a forbidden forest
Where the trees move by their own will
And pilgrims give up all hope.

First Bird Feels a Presence

The presence is with him, not him, but known.
Once in a dream of landscapes, eerie waters,
Things flying about without colors,
It touched him with its eyeless stare,
Told him not to awaken,
To keep on moving through the dense mirror of hours.
Even when talking to rivers
Or hearing voices from the radio about human hunger and respect
He feels this presence, a suppressed howl.
He is supposed to do something with it.
He is pulled into it but it has no path.
He is always entering its outermost orbit,
Its climate of faint whistles, electrical bones.
What would he do if suddenly
It grew a voice, confronted him
Like a playground swing still moving
But nobody moving it.
He is troubled by it, its every form of innocence,
Knows it breathes just beyond death.

First Bird Pushes into the Academy

Pushing into the academy
Bird found himself alone among dead books,
Exhausted authors,
Humor and irony from Ages the print media
Had long since abandoned in the prowl for profit,
Manufactured diseases,
Excellence in high pulp fiction writing.
Among dogs and the heroes
He thought he knew,
He took stock of the questions
That brought him to birth
Amid the fleshy ensemble of veterans,
Executives and pollsters,
Twisting on the pulse of the generation.
Then with a push of his bowels he cleared out the academy.

Bird Returns to Poetry

You return to me beloved,
A dark inheritance, a witch
In search of formulas to reawaken the dead,
A gospel of spring birds,
A musician, briefly deaf,
Suddenly rediscovering sound.
In a burst of memories from childhood you bring sweet berries,
Blue napkins, warm bread and fireflies.
You return,
A rumbling of stallions in the rain
Across a dark and grieving meadow;
A kiss in adolescence awakening to the swoon,
The yeast of bakers,
The throats of poets,
The drone of bees and violas, resonant violins.
Like knots on birch trees suggesting wounds in the forest,
The pure quartz in cathedral stones,
An alabaster singer running through midnight on fire.
Yes
Like the Sermon on the Mount
Delivered in a modern tongue,
You return to me beloved,
Rise upward like smoke in autumn
From blackened leaves, branches surrendered in the wars of
    summer,
Singular, funnel-like, a dark tongue of forbearance
Whispering into the air
Of dragonflies, multiple wings, gift-waves of the Bodhisattvas
Dwelling in light on the inner planes,
Quickening the path from succulence and matter,
Fortitude and fire, through
A blue estuary of desire,
Past every memory of almonds and salt,
Out into the cool and bottomless shadows
Left by the prophets

Extracting bliss from the nerves, the dark wells of the body,
Then abandoning it, like an island
Swallowed up by the sea and death.
You return to me beloved
Ride my breath, my legs, my organs and heart
Through the circus, circumference, the circuitry of days
All the way to the hour when my catalogue, my inference of
    eternity
Is set ablaze in the living presence, the rabid innocence,
That first brought you to me.
Be my lover, let me chronicle you,
Let rivers and stars know your hidden name.
Swim in my blood,
Let me dissolve in you
My astonishing luminous heretic.

Bird Talks to God

When faint, devoid of faith or eloquence,
Your name rises in me,
A feather brushing
Over against my side.
Your eyelash appears as a legend pilgrims confide
To others,
Visiting them alone or in groups,
When there is no more to prove to themselves,
To the fanatical or their families.
Your premonition lights my morning
After nights of fervid dreams or meditation;
Your passing whisper
A pathway through lost violent days.
The suggestion of your presence is enough
To make me again debate the logic of magic;
Your vanishing footprint an entire science
Still to be discovered in an enlightened Age.
A certain kind of music comes with your arrival,
A purer form of glass is bequeathed
When you leave and I am drowned,
Estranged, alone.
A moody form of ecstasy flows through your arms, your irises.
I am beyond love and death when we touch,
When you call my name.

Bird Talking at a Military Funeral

I want to forget the morning
We buried him. I want to forget
The long ride through roses, ashes,
The summer heat like iron,
The numbered plots, serene, ordered,
Flowing in waves through the native grass.
I want to forget
The sentinel music flying overhead
Mixing with flags,
Black testament to fury and loss.
I want to forget the coffin,
Silver tulip slipping underground,
Tears like huge pears,
The mourning flowers rumoring on
In quiet blues about resurrection.
I want to forget the uniformed soldiers
Joining up in his uniform
In the long, downward travel beneath the earth
Toward that imperial stranger embracing us,
Taking all our hidden names,
Astonishments, our discarded bones,
The tender traffic of our news
As we pass like swallows into its breathless entrance.
I want to forget the terror of the leopard,
The blue wine of memory,
The brutal elastic sorrow
In the hydrogen fire of this vessel and life.
I want to know ancestors absorb us,
That we return, like wedding guests, to a familiar
Autumnal forest. I want to touch
The promise of remote angels, secular rivers
Where souls wash, prepare
For vast emergent journeys.
I want to know there are no sergeants or enemies
Before the gate of light,

That we fall, a beautiful fragrance,
Into a mouth of starless immensity.

Bird at a Lynching

When he smelled the carcass from the tree
Burning like carrion of no other
Bird knew he had come to the lowland of souls
At the river's bottom. He knew them. He recognized them
From another life. They had come back to him
From other journeys he was trying desperately to forget.
Was it My Lai or Thermopolis or Goyet caves by the hill of bones
Where he sacrificed burning human genitals,
Hoped the smoke would rise to the gods of fertility and Vampire,
Revive him, psychically, in his own blood,
Make him feel bright,
Confuse his vision of white with light
So he would collapse in on himself, contract, like them,
Loose the radiant halo that rose from the spine
Through the dark fire of inner life, thinner than an optic nerve,
Carrying the force that could lead him beyond all this.
Bird deep down knew everybody   *already* knew this
But was confused by how many paths to the light
One could take,
Get lost in, get frightened, become paralyzed with terror or guilt,
And so not complete the journey,
Become caul wrapped around the diminishing identity of skin.
Then one became the darkness.
Bird left with resolve.
He would demand a hearing in the Great Council Hall
Standing in the shadow of all world governments.
He would plead sublime ignorance,
Declare it all a vast hoax of entangled thoughts and emotions
    spinning
On the outer rim of some nameless creation.
They would believe him.
He would know he was on the path.

Bird Commits Haiku Fifteen Times

1

Cast out from the stars,
Blackened river beyond death,
Yet mortal I fly.

2

In a narrow time,
By the dogs of wind and fate,
This wild life is fed.

3

A robin spies me,
His head rocking side to side.
Both of us can fly.

4

My attention breaks.
This bird with spotted brown wings
Drops through the clear air.

5

O wild, distant birds.
There is a halo coming.
My soul, estranged.

6

Mind, an empty bell,
Vibrations make forms, faces;
Heavens, hells, arise.

7

Statues talk to God,
Time and woodworm work the flesh.
Deathless evils fly.

8

Stranger in the belly,
Eyes of dark and wounded doves.
Days redden my veins.

9

We are ripples now,
Apples, cherries, pass through me.
Waves turn into time.

10

Someone is dying,
A river enters my eyes.
Birds burst into flight.

11

Willows bend like dreams,
Dark necessity follows.
Who will catch the earth?

12

Furious shadows,
The witches are riding me.
Dreams bleed from the moon.

13

Meditating moon,
Distilling the summer sky.
Crickets sing with frogs.

14

The sky is dancing,
I am unable to fly.
Sadness burns my tongue.

15

So many good poems,
Leaves descending in autumn.
Cruel is memory.

Bird's Knowledge

Bird knew his sexual fluids
Were no match for the beauty of god.
So he gathered the animals of his sleep together,
Questioned them one by one
On what they would do if by chance
They encountered the luminous mystery of their appearance here
Among shadows, aphids and the stars of the firmament.
Carpenter ants became his disciples,
But he rejected them, their hosannas, their cries for mercy.
Bees orbited about his head,
As did mosquitos, butterflies,
And the inscrutable loons
With their wailing, fog-deep, elemental songs.
He mastered these wave-fronts where music began,
Unraveled the prophecy of the bats.
When a child asked him why the full moon hung low in the sky
Like a pregnant wolf
About to give birth,
He pointed to the Holy Land,
The halos around the heads of the saints.

Bird's Blessing

Whenever I drink wine of a certain celestial color,
Or meditate on the brutal spirituality of my cat,
I think,
Blessed are the feral, the outstretched, the forgotten.
Blessed is an acorn, the cold receding sky.
Blessed is the frog, who will not survive the winter.
Blessed is the widow, her sex reawakening.
Blessed is the iris, the sharp edges of bone.
Blessed is the holy work of the scalpel.
Blessed is the sculpture dreaming in stone.
Blessed is the incalculable splendor of the morning
When the sun, for no apparent reason,
Is a scarlet wave on the beach
Eviscerating everything standing, seagull to conch shell to
    preacher
Abandoning religions
For the fountainhead of new life.
Blessed is the elemental basis of salt.
Blessed is the leaf self- immolating in autumn.
Blessed is the vibration, the wood burl,
The clear signature of air,
The imperishable authority that brings order to numbers,
To wagons, to sea.
Blessed is the fish, the orbit of Saturn
Within the hollow of its moons,
Ordinary honey dissolving in a glass of tea.
I think of this under a star,
On a far island of the world,
Autumn descending in a black diamond
Into the earth. But I want more,
More than blessedness, more than names, more than forgotten
    diseases.
I want to go beyond cholera,
Beyond the testimony of stars
Carved in glass and iron

Hidden under the rose colored stone tomb, in a forgotten pyramid,
Hundreds of feet beneath the excavated sands
Still undiscovered near the Giza plateau.
I want flocks of ibis birds
Taking to the air, the menacing color of crocodiles,
Rare juices, blossoms of pear and lemon rind,
The faint afterglow of a hummingbird's tail.
I am willing to follow, be a sailor in the Coral Sea,
Freed from the brown arm of circumstance,
Borrowing and paying back money and my debt
With each breath, marking my talent,
Willing to gamble this surgery of the heart
In a river of words extending
Into the punctuation, the liver-dark wisdom of a great howl
Bringing earth nightly to attention,
Surrounded by mercy, extravagance, ragged events.
I am willing to walk, blindfolded,
Into the riddled belly of extinct volcanoes,
Pillars and tongues of petrified lava,
Sulfur with the devil's breath rubbing up against my back.
I am willing to wander the catacombs,
Become lost in flash river floods
Coming suddenly in the desert,
Without apology, violent and alone,
Eating the cacti and spiders burrowing down its path,
Taking them to new, effluvial lands.
But I am surprised, surprised and harassed by the wind,
Surprised that I have forgotten
The secret chemistry between gravity and blood.
I am always walking
Through lifetimes and marriages,
Fugitives and bank accounts,
Through computers, penitentiaries, through the wired world.
I am surprised and blessed
By the deep growl in the of the bell of eternity

That has brought me to awareness of infinity, divine ignorance
 and emptiness again and again.
I am a hollowed salt mine
Waiting to be filled. I am your sister's humor
Mixed with camphor and sadness,
Tangled up with the murmur of the sea.
I am the hat of a beautiful older woman
Discarded after death,
Fading on the shelf of a second hand shop,
Plumed with feathers, shadows, echoes of a previous life,
Leather purses, the heels of worn-out shoes.
All this has turned silent
Running under dead water
Into a distant moan of trains
Carrying wounded soldiers to hospitals from the front.
I will make sacrifices to smoke,
I will take out the backs of my eyes, return them to God.
I will renounce heredity, take my chances
On coming back a saint or goat or small red fish.
Strangers will walk by my tomb.
Blue wings will emerge, affix to their toes.
Always there is this appetite in my heart.

Bird's Revelation

It has been my ambition
To capture the world of illumination in verse,
Smell the hidden consciousness of things,
Abide by the trigger, the sepulcher of my will,
Until truth, like an apple,
Falls by gravity into my hands.
When the animal of my birth
Brings me to autumn,
Every color looted
From the earth,
Skies thicken with migrations to the south,
And bees fully reinterpret the mystery of death.
Black potatoes rot in the fields
And the crows, like shrill priests, call in the morning.
I witness the stars
Dumping their laughter into my dreams,
My computers await a higher intelligence,
And the oral darkness enfolds me in an unseen light.
I break out
Into a murder of birds flowing into air.
Libations, peregrinations of wind,
Grab, go skyward,
In the bright blue of my desire.
With morning,
The dark truth of myself.
I pull myself
Up into the Black Dot, Bindu of creation,
Up through and out the last sutures of the skull to close,
Sealing myself in a cathedral of time and bone.
There is a river here, luminous,
Flowing in slow motion through innumerable dimensions.
Swamps fall into it, into the hands of fisherman,
Into the next morning's moan of battlefields and dogs.
Fruit falls into it,
And the eyes of children not yet born,

And small trees believing themselves a thousand years old,
And the forms angels no longer play with,
And expressions of light dissolving all memory.
Here the Dogon guard the library,
Every book of vibration catalogued, sealed
In the ritual of heartbeat and star
Known to the priests, initiates of Egypt,
Orbiting and impregnated in the dark rites of Sirius
Still on view, gapping and alert,
In the open heart swimming in the skull
Like an ancient sea,
To the dark inner ports of the ventricles of the brain
Where beauty, breath and geometry
Fix in alignments, cast nets,
Track the resonance within us reflected between star and star.

***

If a woman were the sea
She would know this. She would take
The black oyster of my nativity,
Fling it out to her sisters in the distant wind
And wait for the voice beyond death
To bring it back from the salt and religions of fire.
There is a legend that the world is new,
But I know it is old,
Older than shoes cast off by the traveling gods,
Older than sorcery, than pumice,
Than the world behind the world
Where enigmas gather,
Where bold silver streaks out,
Where a cold finger in the weaponry of time
Plunges through stomachs,
Pulling out diseases, out secrets like spoiled intestines,
Coarsening the dream into matter and birth.
I have seen this river before,

Subtle as quince rind,
Moving between blisters that shadows make,
Smelling of brine, the muliebrity of queens,
An olive's excursion into the roundness of the sublime.

                ***

Tell me, when you reach the floor of beauty,
Where shall I stand,
Where shall I encounter numerology, ghosts,
Quantums of evidence known to the stones,
The moody operetta of leaves mixing with snow?
Come with me,
Into the day without licenses,
Day where colors rarely seen
Come back to us, crawl to us,
Hand over hand, smothered in immense solitudes,
Gracious as elk, with the fortitude of boulders
Unearthed by great rivers and glaciers,
Vagabonds of the brute and intolerable
Revealed in the blood of this hour.

Bird Finds a Poem at the End of the World

Naked, without history, no longer afraid of the void,
Bird began walking toward the poem at the end of the world.
He passed the future where gigantic fish
In lurid ponds
Birthed in science and a nightmare of genetics;
He passed historians and their incantations
Singing on the burial mounds of Stalin, Lenin,
The Soviet pantheon
Setting behind glass entombed in wax.
He flew over lakes in Africa,
Past boats on a river in Chad.
He walked on stones toward the mosques of Mohammed,
His shadow still calling. He walked north
Through ice reefs and caverns with the tusks of mammoths
Still unfound.
He walked toward the poem at the end of the earth
Where seas fall, deserts expand and the laws of sacrifice
Spread, unevenly, among peoples of the world.
Arms were gathered in piles,
Set on fire,
Acrid sweet smoke rising into the air.
He passed post offices where letters from the soon to be dead
Began organizing in clusters,
Anticipating the year to come.
He drank wine winding itself into colors,
Then into music, then vanishing
Into starless midnight, birth-whorl in the oval hood of night.
He ran, headlong, into the poem at the end of the world,
Fell into the arms of a dreamer finally
Abandoning her body for the last time,
Her memories becoming libraries, her face a tablet
Where every occasion of ecstasy ever imagined
Was brought up inflamed
Like diamonds from a deep African mine.
They stared at each other, counted each other's toes.

She undressed, slowly,
Gazelles watched them from a distance,
Learning grace and forgiveness
For the violence witnessed on savannahs.
Nightingales emerged from under her arms.
He knew this was an illusion caused by his brain
So intoxicated and near to death,
But he touched her hair anyway, finding
Nothing there except the wind,
The feeling of rivers branching, going in directions
On no ordinary map.
And when her pockets were emptied, completely,
Her hands upturned, inextinguishably bright,
She offered him the poem from the end of the world.

The First Bird Hears Them Coming in A Little Night Music

By a hidden reservoir he found a Bible,
Then a Koran, then a Gita
All translated from an obscure language,
Wrapped in black leaves,
With a faded signature etched in longhand
Drifting off its shoulder spires.
He opened another page.
Each captured him with the strength of a new enemy.
The words stood, just shy of understanding,
Threatening to destroy the earth he knew,
Make headless demons rise,
Swim into his eyes,
Spill through his inner landscape
In a plague infested wind.
This was his clue.
So he founded a new faith,
One that did not *require* his eyes or hands
Or any form of judgment
Not proved by scalpel
Or science
Or witnesses to private crimes
Known only to its practitioners
And the small curving objects they worshipped,
But never viewed.
Quiet and alive, moving,
They lived in a parade under the tilted night stars.
He reached in
Deeper and deeper with each service,
Communion wafers falling from the sky
Like predatory moths swarming the night
Attaching themselves
To his light, trying to climb back, back up into his pineal gland.
There the black-faced gods
Spoke to him

Of the mineral genius of the earth stored up in him
And fed to the travelers
Passing through his bodies, life after life,
Singing to each other,
Merged into the other's souls like husband and wife.

First Bird in a Slipstream
following Hermes Trismegestus

Behind my name,
Behind my language,
Behind my organs, my hands, my veins,
Behind my eyes,
The shadows I move through,
Beneath dreamless sleep,
The darker river of who I am,
Under voices in the stones
I look out at the violent, remote geometry of the stars,
Search for an opening
In the deep belly of a conch shell.
I enter the slipstream
Following matter into form,
Ba bird changeling in a conscious dream.

              ***

Echoes without source,
Dry air and hunger, bones and remains,
The wail of shadows
And homeless men
Come to me, speak in remarkable voices,
Speak with translucent faces,
Speak holding themselves
To the clock on the horizon.
The wide vermillion sun rises,
The earth falls.
Birds of a thousand illegal colors
Sweep in through with the afterglow of a spiritual war.
I fly over alluvial, over primordial lands;
Serpents near waters, crocodiles in mud.
I come to the skull
Of an African warrior
Burned, cracked, heat leaking

From the looting of Thebes,
Sacked libraries older than Alexandria and Troy.
Catching the smoke from an open tomb
I rise, phoenix-like, folding into a tongue,
Tongue becomes a hand, then an eye,
Then a brain dreaming into existence
A whole body that walks, cries,
Calls itself a man.

***

On the shore, in groups of three,
Stand thirty three, splendid ducks.
Three pyramids in the background hold suspended, reflected,
In a pool of sand
Beneath three stars of Orion's belt.

***

Three conscious deaths brought me here.
Three more
And the journey is done.
Suddenly,
An angel with black teeth
And a deformed wing
Flies at me like an rabid bat
Humming, singeing
My one good ear. It sticks its boney wing
Like a wasp's sting into the left side of my belly,
Pulls out an angry fetus.

***

The sky drops its predictions, its reasons,
Its automatic rain
In big black drops. Drops like coal,
Like drums heard in distant mountains.

Drops feeding cities with plague, monsoons,
Rivers of black mud, the threat of typhus.
I push the soul along the shore
Like a drunken gondolier, steer clear of pirates,
Slip around hippos emerging
Like great pigs from the water.
The current picks up. An ibis bird stands.
A familiar silence
Pulls me back into my skull. I forget everything
Again.
The trees, listening, say nothing,
Clouds, like discarded rags,
Fill up the sky.

First Bird in an Open Field

Going black
The first bird stands in an open field.
His legs hold to the ground, frightened, shaking,
Watching as the dark legends push up
From a punished place inside the earth.
He doesn't believe in hell,
Says so repeatedly when asked, when singing.
Still he fears the echo
Rumbling,
A terrible distant music, a little like Wagner,
Comes across the field. What should he do?
The trees shiver, crows grow silent,
Blond wigs appear out of nowhere.
Suddenly it begins to rain and the music rises
Like a flood.
He decides to take precautions,
Injects himself with the sap from a mysterious nearby tree
That has lived for over a thousand years,
Largely unnoticed, being small and fruitless.
Sexual poetry comes from this.
A song about the final days of the Roman Empire suggests itself
In the way the leaves flutter about him
As the sun goes down.
He worries about creativity.
He worries the earth may open more and more
Until Himmler, Hess and the other mole men of the Waffen SS
Stage a return to glory, outlaw his blood.

Bird Talks to the Rain

Don't lie to me.
I know you're a prophet
Bringing new life to wastrels and all those beings
Riding fire engines into the flaming sunsets of the world
Where the gods exhibit themselves
To human beings over and over
Refueling the power of religions to invent.
This creates hope if you know what I mean,
If you know what to look for.
I will do what you do,
Throw myself
Into the new economy of the earth.
I will ride a train all night
Through the backdraft of my memory
Until it takes me back to the nineteenth century.
I will pivot and rotate freely
When I hear the stars behind my back
Calling to me to midnight walks.
And if that does not work
I will take the hand of the first vowel that comes to me,
Transmute it,
Turn it into an elegant summary
Of the four fundamental equations
That hold truth, matter and infinity together.
One time, while I lay sleeping
On a Saturday midwinter night,
The rain changed the whole direction of my dreaming.
I slid like a slick moon
Across the sky
That should have been watery with a slight touch of blood.
There were birds everywhere.
Nobody felt safe.
Suddenly, suddenly like a hidden knife
The rain became a howl of black voices,
Then trees shivered with tiny leeches.

Then a sinkhole opened
Into the center of the void
And Alice of Wonderland came out smiling,
Licking her bloody fingernails.

Bird After the Meal

Bird lay on the floor wondering
If the worst was over,
If what was left of his organs
Would seep through the stained carpet
To the apartment beneath him
Where the last bits of the thanksgiving feast were scattered on the table,
The mice waiting until midnight
To gamble their courage for bits of bread,
Dreaming of pools of thick brown gravy.
The game was on T.V. He thought he recognized
One of the players from an old high school photograph
He found last Saturday morning taking trash to the dump.
He was searching through the lost and found shed
For old books, discarded classics.
In a yearbook, half opened, with ketchup stains
On the folded over page
He had seen it, clear as day,
Officious and full of portent. Overhead
The sky debated rain,
Lightening sandwiched between clouds
In the distance.
Returning home he poured himself a glass of chardonnay
He didn't need
Into what used to be a jelly jar that he would later fill
With unmatched screws, rusting nails.
He walked past the bathroom sink
Pondering the bright mystery
Of his common existence here.
When the phone rang
It was his old high school friend,
Wet and crying
Looking for a loan they both knew
He would never repay.

Bird & Colleagues Make a Suicide Assessment

All the dark ones listened.
'Slow down', the spirits said,
'We are discussing suicide
Among the soon to be dead and those whose skulls are constantly

Leaking light.' 'We are guardedly optimistic
That you may be reborn
As an elusive phantom running through the fields
Naked, joined at the hip by hope

Perused by command hallucinations.' Be quiet.
All your knives have been put away,
Your mirrors given back to the stars.
We will replace your name with a diagnosis.

Fortunately for you the demons burrowed in our ears
Are on good terms with one other.
Biblical verses will massage you in the dark.
There is a high probability that if you wade,

Waist deep, into the open sea
An octopus will sweep into your bathing suit like underwear,
Confusing your arousal with sensations of the sea.
Clearly your religion is not the problem.

                              ***

We believe in the war effort of the angels against the crows.
We each have a unique pair of wings.
We share an apocalyptic vision involving chocolate
And waves of women moored in their sleep like graceful ships

Rising, falling, oriented outward toward the great waters.
O we know you would never burn your child.
Down the street a group of disgruntled apostles
Talk about what to do with you

Now that their Savior has married
Leaving them stranded
Like over-medicated patients in the backwards.
You use narcissism like an insulin pump.

You dream of being free, beautiful,
Traveling in schools like striped bass. Yes, we have talked about
    our books
Far too long. Nevertheless a careful questioning
Will reveal the death threats you get come from the dolphins and
    whales.

After the hurricanes pass
We will all gather on the outer banks
Where the sea has forgotten your psychosis
From the other day. We will concentrate, pray,

Withhold nothing from the faceless gods.
We will not lie about your future
Or conjure up imaginary genitalia. Our warm eyes
Will indicate we have done well.

There is no shame in crying
Before a thing of great beauty. We drink heavily,
Hold on to our nostalgia for the sublime.
Despite all this

What if indeed, as you say, we do change identity death after
    death;
What if the trees, bewildered, isolated,
Come back winter after winter,
With a different story ? There is a gentle assumption

In the bones that all of this will pass,
The clouds will clear, that the recurring behaviors of the earth
Require no other signature than Spring.
Our archives are full of such devious propositions.

The First Bird Searches for Beauty.

Leering out of his one good eye
The first bird decided
The earth was bereft of beauty.
So he sucked out the color of a carrot,
Inflamed it,
Then stretched and bent it over the sky
Above those scarlet cauls
That appear, habitually, when sunsets
Invade islands in the south pacific.
It was not enough.
Pulling from the leather strap around his throat
All the menace he could from whips and harnesses,
He twisted them into massaging fingers,
Then crawled with them on his knees for months
Over stones and splinters rumored to be relics of the original cross.
It was insufficient.
He extracted the final love letters of poets
Who perished in suicidal fires of unrequited love,
Read them aloud over the radio,
At bus stops in front the homeless,
At the funerals of young boys who had never tasted sex.
This proved inadequate, vain,
All the while his appetite waning, his feathers growing thin.
In desperation
He jumped into a truck careering recklessly down a one way
        street,
Skimming off the curbs,
Leaving black marks, bits of asphalt scattered
Like kernels of burnt popcorn, hard and useless,
A rancid smell, smoking like oblivion.
Still beauty refused to stop at his doorstep.
So he devised one final sinister plan.
Loaded with weapons
And blood syntrafused from alien bodies
He added a little rock salt, a tincture of caffeine,

Skin excised from newly discovered animals
Found desiccated in the Petrified Forest.
In fury and humiliation
He cast them in a net across the lower frontiers of the universe,
Dragged back in all he had discarded for years;
Scars from weddings,
His goldfish gone belly up when it died,
Excuses from the surgeons
When things went badly.
Beauty then emerged from his bed with a moist handkerchief
And turned to him
Releasing from her heart a fleet of crows
Who fled across the southwest
Through eerie skies
Spreading the gospel that made prairie dogs stand erect,
The ghost of Mary Magdalene relax her thighs.

First Bird Convalescing

When his eyes were removed by the great surgeon
He could see the lost planets of his youth, their atmospheres discarded,
Their rare flora and fauna in the forests on full display
For his analysis and taxidermy experiments.
When they told him about his stomach, how the useless cells had been replaced
By silica and more enduring products
He thanked them for their expertise, their handling of subtle explosives,
Their way with carving out only the visible spots
Where the camera barely reached and the skin would grow back over decades.
When he heard about the bones, the need for adjustments,
The clever prostheses for the finger joints,
He was relieved, even happy, that science had come so far
So incredibly fast since the days of the swinging towers,
The electricity from the storm,
The hopping muscles of the frog's legs
Sliding across the surface on the dissecting room table
With a subtle touch from the scalpel.
All would be well
As he lay on the bed, nurses swimming by like automated saints,
The blood bags at his feet
Filling with his elixir going from red to pink to clear.

The First Bird Overhears Rumors

From the most beautiful of the constellations
He deciphered the secrets of his bloodwork,
What made the animals sing at night,
Why the moon abandoned them for darker lovers behind the
 clouds.
When he tripped and fell running from the plague
He heard that pestilence was a metaphor
Devised to obscure the fact
That he himself was all energy and ovulation in time.
When he understood that he was stationary, that dreams flew
 around him,
He knew for certain
At the bottom of the great ocean there vibrated an immense bell.

The First Bird Grows More Suspicious

When the other birds met secretly
Without him, under logs, in hollowed out caves,
Their voices low, whispering
About his fetishes, his half healed wounds;
When the cloud formations ran
Towards bats, ravens, pterodactyls flying from the local museum,
All rivals for his stunning creations;
When the seas went dark
And strangely quiet
Despite their storms and rabid sunsets
Reported obsessively on the evening news;
When his own beak refused to open,
Worms gyrated suggestively before him knowing they would not
    be swallowed whole
Like cherry tomatoes or those oysters at parties
In the last century;
He felt the corners of his universe shrink
Like a wet paper bag,
Gutters fill with leaves and salt.
So he began to study the science of possession,
The shapes of methane gas above the bogs and marshes at night
When the lights come on, the mysteries are reenacted,
And the strangers from the UFOs approach him with their ridicu-
    lous questions.

Bird's Dream

One winter morning bird could not find his way
Out of a dream.
So he went in another direction, one offering evidence
Of his earthly survival behind a door opening immeasurably
    inward
Toward a dark and steep corridor through windy spaces
Occupied by time and small unnamable beasts.
He did not have to abandon his senses of taste or logic
Or any of the other neurons that wove his mind together
With its original clocks, its vibrating mannerisms.
He reached into a small pocket under his left wing
Where he kept his secrets in a bag. He pulled out a knife,
Then a broken piece of someone else's beak
Discarded on a dark road where once he gotten drunk
After an embarrassingly long but tragic love affair.
He was not far from the canal where he had tried to drown
    himself.
He almost panicked when, reaching further,
He pulled out a small glowing skull of himself
That seemed to describe in low inscrutable tones
How he could fly over the canal
And take in a whole new view of middle earth.
He could even offer the earth a new mythology,
One based on a serenity of symbols
That everyone would know intuitively by their own birthright
And there would be wealth and wisdom for all.
Understanding this
He assumed the correct yogic posture, stood on his head,
His tailbone to the sky. It opened.
Then he flew out of his dream.

Bird in Therapy

When the whole of the celestial equator fell into his lap,
Owls flew from his navel,
Diamonds materialized inexplicably under his wings.
Bird's feathers were spiritualized,
Whiter than rice.
His soul rose, a great beast from sleep.
He moved around in the chair,
Insights from his black plumage falling like leaves
Full of holes filling with tiny immutable secrets,
Each one connected to the next.
His doctor had one good eye on the left side of his head
That turned round and round, every truth coming out
Hitting the bull's eye, causing the spine to go spastic,
The belly fill with gel.
The whole arrangement of organs from liver to spleen
Roiled like an orchestra tuning itself, off key,
Awaiting a conductor
Who would never arrive.
Bird called in, cancelled his next appointment.

The First Bird Makes a Confession

Bird thought,
When the apples fall in autumn
It is my fault, my working with gravity and envy,
Trying to pull them permanently to earth
From their higher tendency to rise up from seed
Toward deeper roots in the constellations.
When it rains and flooding begins again
It's me spilling the innards of heaven
Trying to understand, and then steal the liquid beauty of god
For myself,
Hide it in a nursery, then later ride it through oblivion.
When the churches are burned, mosques incinerated,
Temples closed for indefinite repairs,
It is myself whispering into the ears of sleeping devotees
That all the other religions are full of fornicating demons and
      serpents
In a Sabbath of unbelievers,
Our faith in peril, that we twist over a cauldron of acid.
When the heart suddenly stops on the operating table
It is me flying in low to investigate the moment between one beat
      and another.
I want to know how far away the mind can go from the body
And still make it back to this side of life.
And when the fish is caught, eyes wide and glistening,
The deer shot, gutted in the woods,
The priest no longer listening,
The final gamble fixed,
It is me leaking from the stars
Following light into the forms of matter,
Sewing up the openings between death and birth,
Until the witnesses are satisfied, the jury made its decision,
And the hooks of Eden removed from all the guests.

The First Bird Receives a Vision

'Vision is seeing what isn't seen'
My friend confessed to me
Who is ailing from cancer. I took what he meant
Past the heart into the dreams I swam into
Over the next three days or so.
Surrounded by breath and a new body
Born in a different river of matter and time
I saw how each tissue of spacetime
Enfolded every moment of creation
In Ages yet to be;
Around the earth's core rotational axis
Our future bodies sleep;
Each quantum being seen splitting into a different universe.
And my work, my future work, fixing the broken wobble of the
    earth
Set off in a galactic conflagration
By some other's deep mammalian urge.

Bird Stares into the Mirror

He saw an Asian face and trembled,
An African face, screamed;
He pulled a face from under the Ural Mountains
Shuddering
Until black ink drained from his feet.
His tongue contracted, retreated to its cave.
All his gargoyle cousins
Fled back atop their cathedrals,
Watched over the canals
As the bodies floated by
Moved along from the bottom by the current
One by one, like shiny coins,
Into the pocket of a great thief.

Bird Reading His Entrails

Bird waved his wing in front of the smoky mirror
Calling forth light.
But out came his past life as a trilobite, *then a fish*,
Then a more advanced reptile,
Then a small creature crawling through the brackish dark.
He looked for home, comfort, for whatever promised him that
    someday he could fly.

***

He went back to sleep.
The next night he covered himself with armor,
Focused his courage and semen up along his spine.
He ran through the darkness this time,
Promised to take no prisoners from his intimate mythology
Or the dreamers he found littered along on the roadside,
Heading west, into the summers only the dead can see.
Amethyst crystals condensed around his claws.

***

On another try he called out to his father,
To the sacred journey they shared
Toward the god of the great phallus
Who lay sleeping in the depths of the cave that locks its doors
    after you enter.
He woke in a night sweat.
It dawned on him that he was dying,
Taking with him all that his ancestors had ever embodied
Down to the bottom of an ancient lake
Where the lamprey is nobly sweeping through the depths.

***

Flying toward his 70th year
Trailing with failed books
And the knowledge that he was an immortal soul

Shredding its body on reefs
And small conversations,
Suddenly his astonished bones stood up,
Bore witness to pure carbon,
Bottomless eyes,
Applications from those who died in childbirth
To return to life,
To swoon in the science connecting their DNA
With the swirl of planets
A hundred thousand light years beyond Alpha Centauri.

Bird Gives Away Parts of His Body

To the ice age he gave his legs,
Then his arthritic wings,
Releasing them into rivers moving with wooly mammoths
And white tusks of remorse,
His toes and ankles bent,
Thickened with the weight of his thighs.

    ***

To the sky with its bulging hot eye
He gave his fingernails so that other birds
Might see themselves reflected, opaquely,
Like ghosts confused in their passing through the last sudden
 death.

    ***

To the noise of tire wheels
Seeming to come from his breath
He gave a long exhausting squeal
Like a pig knowing the hot skin-searing showers
Come next.

    ***

To the religious garage where his heart was kept
He surrendered the windows, the car keys, the tool boxes
Serving the organs and their replacement parts
Dreamed up by his brain during its consultation with the
 surgeons.
His skull was to be auctioned, at cost,
To the Daughters of the American Revolution
In exchange for a copyright
On who is a *real* American and who is not,
Along with a full list of names of those slipping across our south-
 ern borders at night,
Hiding out in the kitchens

Of the dearly beloved.

***

The rest, the metatarsals, the brown lava of the liver,
The long hammer, anvil and stirrup burrowed deep in the ears
Are left to scavengers and speculators
Who can store them
In the jars of refrigerated rooms, behind clinical doors,
Locks triple threaded, the noise low and humming
Like the inside of an expensive jet.

Bird's Final Failure on Earth

He came to the riverbank where they were hiding
With all their diseases and wires.
Without holding hands or whispering they understood
The marriage of birds, the wind sweeping above their heads
In small circles
And the way the leaves would have to push out again from the
    branches
When their time came.
The hour seemed perfect.
He brought together all his sense organs;
Eyes, for the night peering endlessly into the dark;
Nose, for the new prairie of animals with their small intuitions
    about death;
Ears, to guide his long evacuation underground
Relying exclusively on echoes, vanishing apparitions
Bouncing off the walls;
Skin, for the pure magic of feeling;
And taste, so he would not have to lie to Jesus again or explain
All the reasons for the nocturnal baptisms.
He lifted his right wing
And a memory of the great flood returned;
He pulled back.
He listed, by name, all the dismembered soldiers from World
    War II;
They heard him but pretended not to hear,
Bent down, tied their shoes.
It was getting dark, so he spoke of the stars as fires,
A candelabra over the body of god;
They shared opinions about deodorants,
Who could pee farthest in the backyard.
He was getting nowhere.
So he showed them the right side of his pubic bone,
Scares from the operation;
They wanted to know about the overflow of silt into the Indus
    valley.

In a panic
He told them about the Wizard of OZ, his arrest,
His subsequent confinement; they made a ribbon
Out of the tongues of his enemies sewn together, their own and
    the Pope's.
Then he stood on a table and screamed
'According to our current understanding of the laws of physics
It is illegal to fly headfirst
Through the center of the Milky Way
And emerge at the feet of the prophets writing the chronicles of the
    species
Within us
Not yet born'; they turned on the radio, listened for skip
    frequencies
Howling between the stars.
Finally exhausted, perplexed,
The staples bursting from his organs,
He tried again to have them walk barefoot and naked
Across the cosmic fire;
'Do you realize we are mutating,
Each of us,
From element to element, our wills, our most intimate secrets
The property of owls, vagabonds, worshipers of the night birds
Who live in the trees all day calculating where their prey will be
When the moon descends
Within the hollow spaces of the earth?;
That the cattle watching us with wide eyes
Behind the fences fully understand but will never speak?;
That the womb of Magdalene, opened by the surgeons in cesarean
    section,
Successfully sued
The angels of death for the most luminous skulls of Golgotha?'
They clipped their toenails, collected them in a bag,
Offered them to him.

Bird in a Flashback Recalls Himself a Constellation

Since the love of god was innate with him
Blindness did not matter.
He was pulled across vast expanses
Like all the others
Toward the Great Attractor.
Evil lost its nerve in the passage,
Ambition collapsed like lint in a navel.
He remembered his mother,
How the cracked egg damaged her so badly.
Without cunning, without gravity,
Without the coiling directives from his gizzard
Out of which he drew all the primal questions
Wine was now softer than a child's ear
When it went down his throat.
He recalled the last supper,
The insults from Judas,
How Magdalene was not invited,
How he turned into a small lizard on the wall
That no one else could see. He thought himself
An apostle sent back
Gathering what had been left in his master's shadow.
Then he flew on into the lightning beyond light.

The First Bird in Flight

On and on he flew
Redefining death and beauty
Until he fell into the sea beneath sleep...

Bird Recalls When His Voice Returned To Him

When my voice returned to me,
When I lay on the bed, unable to categorize, to label
The sheer violence of the fish, the animal feeling,

The black pond of memories
Sweeping through me
To reach this hour, hour

Unthreatened by primal terrors or instruments with thorns,
Or knives used in wars
Holding back things from the river of images moving beneath my
    sleep;

When I pulled in my net
From the florid sea,
Full of great eyes, narratives of the coral,

Birds of the night forests, music of the quantum,
The rhythms of the heartbeat;
When I returned, naked, from the public fire of attention,

Soul bathed in rickets,
Praise, the fury of religious bigots,
Strangled alive in the editorials of the exiles

Wandering the virtual spaces of the new economy;
It was then, then I called back, took my own hand,
This hand, this wing, no different from the hand of someone

Ten thousand years ago,
Or ten thousand years from now,
Or ten thousand light years from here,

In another time-fold spinning in orbit
Around the inhabited stars
Of spiritual siblings

Beyond the outer rim of Taurus and Alpha Centauri.
My voice, pilgrim and witness of bodies,
Wove through me even though I had not deciphered

Its liquid equation of immortality
Working its way through my bone-stuff and breath.
I know this and you know this.

In us an intimate mathematics is striving to be born;
A codex describing the symbols our bodily organs mean
In the sea of energy swimming below us, surrounding the atom,
    singing in the strings

We are beginning to hear
In the outstretched reality winding toward us.
I survive the fall of every object

Pulled from the upper world of insight and beauty.
I meet every sorrow as a small ocean
I cross over

To reach myself hidden in you,
In the mood of children,
In the swamp of forgetfulness we become lost in during grief

In our pioneering years
Wading through the conversations of strangers,
The endless bargains we make making a living.

I have moved away from things I recognize
In pursuit of pure direct ignorance;
I touch again

The original poem of creation falling out of my hands at birth,
Rolling across the floor,
Taking up residence

In smoky mirrors that have not released all their light

Despite the promised axioms of science.
I take sunlight personally.

I assume the sound of waterfalls
Is meant for me,
Mixing with the rain,

Suggesting things I am wholly inadequate to understand
In the prison of reason, bodily senses,
Tongues so obscure they are only heard as myth

Or hypnotic fire.
The moon is the source of lunar desire
Splicing verbal and femoral currents together

In the night wings folding around lovers
In conversations, kissing, thrusting under bed sheets
From Mumbai to Cape Town

To the smaller outlets and bays along the coasts
In sea towns from the Carolinas to Maine.
There are bees droning on about matter and death,

Brutal symmetries discovered between ourselves and those we
    hate,
Narrow epistemologies we must interpret unless we go insane
Trying to imagine a fate

More course, more salt-like
Than the graves of sailors
Lost to the waves and journeys

Taken long ago
In ships with names existing only in forgotten languages.
They live on the edge of antiquity's memory

Fall inward
Like my earliest memories of flight and death.

You and I are incomparable equals, cohabit

The same stern territory out of which dreams are lifted,
Carried from one place to another
Beyond the juncture of mineral and element

Into the space of pure sound
Every melody, every rhythm seeks to quote
In the harvest of chord, vibration and pitch.

There are hollows in the burls of woods
Still growing
Seeking us out, calling us to mold them into purer shapes

Whose meaning is elliptical,
Known by touch,
Dangerous to the intellect, agnostic of color.

There are narratives, fables of strong women
Who swim, mindless, out into the winter's tidal pools,
Worshipping gods,

Drawing energy from folds in space
Connecting distant worlds together
Without the use of religion or space-time, only the catechism of
    beauty

Passing through the elusive wine of human flesh.
If we wandered together,
Just the two of us,

We would see around us, in air, among the stones,
Hidden in the shifting shapes of grass,
Other walkers, other riders of waves in the centuries

Before and after us,
Touching the Agni, the first fire, the corpse and sprouting flower
Encasing the beginning and end of the bodily drama,

Animating its hands, heating its belly,
Driving through the wreck and fountain
Toward the book of common vessels

The angels hold, pass verses through from mind to mind.
I have slid off the edge of a dream
To meet you here.

I stand naked and watery,
An undulating root and soul,
Suspended in the warm fathomless ocean of your presence,

Hoping to be seen by *your* soul, *your* mirror,
Your dark inspiration for what is cavernous in us,
For what is poignant, equilateral,

Capable of translation,
The most obedient of all the theorems of God.
My neurons bow to wonder and awe.

Every fact I know is disciple to a higher order,
Changing plans only
In the face of what is more luminous, more spacious, more egalitarian, more subtle

And sublime.
There is no way to know
How long we live after death

In the mouths, the names of those we loved and who loved us.
There is no hour we know we loved deepest,
The rest being shadows of that luminous moment.

There is no echo we hear.
When our eyes close,
We fall through the skin,

Head for seas in which all sailors, all admirals are equals,

Where mermen and mermaids
Reveal themselves resonate, our more articulate brothers,

Riding on a different evolutionary arc,
Who sense the seas *beneath* form and the flow of coarse matter,
Travel currents between the greater and less stars.

I sing the body *beyond* the body,
The body not menaced by medicine and psychiatry,
Not stagnating in vestibules of the protectors of the faith.

I sing the *light body* breaking through
Death after death
We find easily, unremarkably, in the hands of small children

Grasping for the moon or their mothers
Or early colors pulling at their eyes, whispering that dogs and cats
Have souls, that water is alive,

That butterflies live in trees that help them change clothes
And fly out again with a new face
Yet are still the same companions seen

Drifting across the summer grass
Returning in the wind a prodigal, an errant boy,
A delicious apple transforming into a bird

With the secret word
That trails off in a dream.
I sing the body beyond the body

Surrounded by phalanxes of trivia, corporate news, false disclo-
    sures of failing banks,
Reptiles in the garden, sink holes in the bedroom
Swallowing us whole,

Nuclear proliferation for only the white or wealthy boys of the
    earth,

Obscene and bottomless 'third world debt.'
Over and over moving through my right ear, then my left,

The male geography, the female lakeshores,
The swell comes toward me, greets me, pulls and demands and
    pleads with me
Not to be afraid,

In the age of clever atheism and glass,
To sing of the immortality of the soul,
The body behind the dense body,

The body riding between stars in the solar ambience,
Outlawed by science
Embarrassing to religion,

Consigned to poetry, to flash witnesses in dreams of the dead
Who call back to us in our straightjackets of 'hard data.'
The breath of our first fathers moves in me,

The milk and thigh
Bequeathed by our original mother
Sings to us in tongues dissolved in a trillion hours of change

Mutation and migration across timescapes,
Histories swallowed up in oral books,
Living moist in the throats of Griots,

Ambulating through daydreams when, on automatic pilot,
We drift through museums devoted to 'primitive peoples,'
The delusions of the gifted, the beautiful,

And those drowning in pools of their own voices and magic.
Over prairies I have not yet traveled, over the homesteads of those
Not yet born,

I walk, whisper freely of what I have seen, what has come to me,
What I confess and own and write down

Before my death

And return to flight.
Invite me into the luminous circle of your imagination,
Into the edge of what you remember

But are too frightened to declare in the days of tires, money
And financial canopies hanging over us in jobs, respectability,
What our rational colleagues will say

About regression to childhood, Paleolithic thought,
To promises squandered in pursuit of what never was,
What can never be.

Come, lets us gather, both of us,
Into this sudden moment of insight and change.
If we do this

We will enter the city that knows all our names,
Knows the incantations we hear in our sleep,
Knows we are not exhausted by beauty

And will not waver in the face of inexplicable grief.
I am ashes and roses, I know,
And so are you

Whose heart is an elliptical orbit around truth.
If we trust ourselves, if we lift our arms at night,
We will find them attached to galleons,

Ancient galleons,
Galleons pushing deep into the world of salt and oceans we travel
Heading each time into a new port

Where the body is reborn,
Where the day and our memories are slightly adjusted,
Accommodating what is necessary, what is correct.

Diving deeper into the waters
We come across cathedrals
Sunken long ago

When the city they arose in sank under the weight of war,
Cataclysmic upheavals.
Great fish swam in and out of abandoned windows,

Seaweed undulates from catapults, from pews where the faithful
Once swayed to dense and enormous music.
Look out with vast eyes.

See how fate has chosen us
From among the creatures
Given to self-consciousness and desire.

We surrender into gratefulness,
Renounce unnecessary habits,
Acquire tools allowing us to peer deeper into God

Doing the work among strangers and children
Learning the root of all language.
I am in debt for the voyage of small sinners.

I could not be happier knowing
My innumerable imperfections accumulate
And are translated.

I approach the mornings, sometimes ill, sometimes well, a gambler
Throwing instinctively the right dice.
Forgive the unwise, they too are imperishable,

And their sleep is not as restful as yours.
Do not hide from them the knowledge of the great river within the
          river
Flowing through them, their lungs, their bloodcells, their breath.

They do not see,

But inherit equally as you and me.
Come and go through the apothecary of the body,

Through gates swinging open,
Closing, the wings of a gorgeous butterfly
Drunk with the nectar of summer

When sun, intoxicated with air
And clouds, forms balconies
In an avalanche of color

Not restrained, without breaking things,
Unfolding new forms of beauty
That would take thousands of years to give proper names.

Release your breath, your tongue,
Your memory of being curled up in the body
With its entrances and exits,

Its hiding places for the secret rituals of birth and death.
Be free of embodiment.
Let this be the last summer you touch earth

As a calculus of organs, bones,
Bits of tooth.
Let your hair be no more than the sway of trees, or the brush of
    cacti,

Or the necessary covering of hills.
Be the original poem of the blood,
Salt and sweet, evasive, a shy animal

Moving between unseen places and meadows,
Beneath the stones, above crystals, beyond the squadron of the
    nightjars
Who marry themselves

To the vision of boys, rude and intemperate in their own dreams,

Drifting out of windows, through the branches,
Out into the skies stretching over long valleys

Where the blue modest birds are heard daily
In their haunts, their quiet nests.
I am unwritten,

Unquotable as the air, as the scarlet after-spill of the day
Chasing the bleeding gods west into the underworld.
Here the dark things of the earth live,

Rise, meet us in the shadows
We turn from but are always pulled back toward
In our search for inward, unspeakable grace.

If I could roll the entire world into one,
If I could reflect in my words
A fragment of the truth

Held in a dead skin cell sloughed off from the body
In a morning's shower
I would be closer to what passes wordlessly

Between you and I.
I remain unscripted as I navigate the air
And its two currents come back together when I pass.

On some days
I dream the sea lost its way, created
Then abandoned me on this shore to fend for myself

Among objects of pain, confusion, desire and sorrow.
The death of children, prisoners, people without money or health
Fill my mind some days

And I am distracted, wholly unable to cooperate or comprehend
What is happening to me.
I sense I am a body, newly emerged from the river

Forgotten by science and machinery,
Skin shimmering with the resonance rain leaves
Over ponds and pavements of flagstone in gardens

Neatly arranged by hands rooted in geomancy,
The deepest intuitions of telepathy and fire.
The oldest human soul is an African soul.

I reach back and touch it,
The warmest covenant between mother and child,
The foundation of insight, the well of awe

Echoing up
And inhabiting our bones.
And then again sometimes I sense I am an autumn leaf

Traveled to this world
Drunk with color and death
Folding back into the soil of infinite migration.

I don't know if a child
Has a deeper vision than this,
If a dog has any sense of criminal behavior,

If exuberance and ecstasy is the common talk of sunflowers
When they see each other standing tall, legislative,
Over fields undulating in the wind

Under the summer sky.
I have buried and resurrected myself many times in this life.
I have found my tongue where alphabets and dictionaries wither

And mirrors become great hollows
Out of which birds swim toward me
Then beyond

Whispering they will never die.
When finally I am washed of knowledge

I walk straight into the afternoons,

Each object suggesting its own dissolution, its own rebirth.
What I am trying to say,
Why earth has brought me here,

Is that poetry is a science of mind riding
Many roads at once, mixing the matrix of things,
Where a toenail is the signature of the long march,

And the simple grass the antennae into the world
For beings and intelligence
Outside our dimension, curious

Of the green and watery passions
We weave, live in and ride our currents through
Until we too are revealed as the outward foam in the ocean of
    God,

Constantly in flux, roaming from form to form
With time and matter, the names of children
Rolling like dice and sea babble

In a swirling glass.
Come what will, come what may,
I enter death a million times and say to my colleagues

I am not embarrassed I vanish
Nightly before my own eyes
And wake up astonished by the mystery

Behind the cycle of sleep, the biochemistry, the elaborate
    syncopation
Between myself and the stars
Everyone breathes, calls by different names, marks in the coil of
    our DNA.

One day

When my entire electricity is summoned up
I will approach perfection enough to sail, with a full invitation,

Into the lunar pulling of waves,
The invisible matrix of things
Promised by the bishops of my childhood,

Their hands folded, their eyes careering upward,
Their cassocks and ancestry
Calling back *deeper* than Magdalene and her young apprentice on
    the shores of Galilee.

I will stop changing religions
Like bloodcells depleted of iron.
I will feel trees open their roots under the earth.

I will lie nightly
Beneath the pond of the sky,
Watch stars drift like faint swans over the surface

Heading toward the Great Attractor out of sight,
Beyond hearing and darkness,
Skimming distant rims with an exuberance of forms and
    consciousness.

The First Bird Returns To Flight

"I am one of those Spirit-souls who dwell in the Light-god."
Chapter LXXVIII- Chapter on Changing into a Divine Hawk
Papyrus of ANI/Egyptian Book of the Dead

i

Bird's Egg Song

How do we come to be?
I don't mean sex and sperm and voluptuous egg,
But that other life,

Life of light and intelligence,
Oceans of radiance, dark harbors,
Pledges to the earth pulling us into

Fingernails and nerves,
Calling to places, sirens,
The ringing of deep bells,

The current of voices in languages heard
Beneath sleep,
Remote geographies, the warmth of breeding, the deep thalassic
    migrations.

In the winds around me
Swim the breath of poets, their extinguished songs,
Their almanacs, their incandescent words,

Swept up into the coiling of my ear.
I have no gift for translation,
Am ignorant of history, of the syntax bringing them,

Like opulent fruits, exquisite wines,
To the bone-white shore of attention.
Poets speak in black tongues,

Burn their own books,

Release their breath into rising smoke,
Ride the tailwinds back into hills filled with angry forgotten gods;

Poets outlive their sons,
Die of pestilence, skin lesions,
Concocted cures for imaginary diseases

Roaming the sense organs
Smelling for the blood, the oil, the meat.
I am just another fallen angel,

A crude fly
Stuck in this tissue of space-time and desire.
But the first bird was a poet,

Pure signal, a single flame,
Lifting above forest,
Beyond stationary stones,

Past the ambient sea,
Living deeper than the limbic system,
The scales of the dogfish, the curl of the past

With its sleek academy of whales,
The crushing depths of starfish, mollusk, falling inward, then
Spinning out further than the Pleiades and Mars.

He sang *'dark forces rule over*
The earth',
That *'death is a narrow bridge spiraling,*

Connecting souls from life to life'.
He sang his allegiance to high windy places,
Angles of ascent, communion, absorption in the triangular spaces
　　　above the head.

He sang from memory of a celestial race,
Of beings *above* light

Their footprints flowing down into beauty, insight and thought.

Once, just once, falling into the lower mirror of life,
He saw a black crow
Fumbling for a cigarette,

A robin bleeding with discomfort
Sliding into the silver of his age,
An egret sulking, wanting more money,

A vulture picking at bones,
A nightingale, denuded of feathers,
Slowly and inexorably

Putrefying into a bat. Smelling this
He left the bodily outer ward of his existence,
The hill of flies and mold,

Flew out over the sutra of waves
Pulled by endlessly opening insight. Stitching together
A song of membranes,

A calyx of syntax, order,
A baffling orgy of tongues
That gave him speech

He delivered it intact to Congress,
Was rewarded with suspense, beneficence,
Awesome applause.

Over the din of voices, hosannas,
Came calls for even more. Then in me
The first bird rose, sank, glided down,

Lead bombardier running out of fuel,
Engine sputtering, bullet holes everywhere,
Heaving with gravity into matter and life.

ii

The Way of the World He Saw

Suddenly, suddenly the blue interior of heaven
Spilled out.
Angels who had lost their way from the war appeared to him,

Innumerable wasps spreading stings.
Next came the blind scholars,
Then the bloodied priests, then the novelists,

Then the official mummifiers of the body
Lying in wait for the next Pope.
None of this escaped the other birds,

Or the fishermen,
Or migrant workers in the open fields
Who had stopped for lunch.

By late autumn
The kingdom of fallen leaves,
Glistening like black otters in the rain,

Had moved in with the wind
Covering the earth with broken fingers
Before all went sheer black.

The first bird,
Reawakening through
Generation after generation of wings

Walked among the piles, looking left, right,
Victorious admiral floating above the battle, the wounded.
The empire of fire was his.

The arms, the bones and the eyes were his.
The obelisk revolving in the center of the skull was his.

Snowflakes fell,

Infinitesimal parts;
A stupendous chandelier exploded, scattered and spent itself
Over the cold of the earth.

        iii

His Blood Vessel Song to the Great Attractor

"Sublime One,
Bring your heart to me
A beautiful river,

A minor god,
A tongue of basil and salt filling
My cavities, reminding me of the sea.

Burning, a relic cured in ancient fires,
A message in tomatoes, forks,
Knives sharp enough to cut through the moon.

Seabirds adrift, searching for sanctuary
Becoming lions and fists
Struggle for strength in my clumsy memory and imagination.

I bring them closer.
I land, air in great circles,
Catch myself in the water and wind

Surrounding you. I look, fist and bone,
To be part of you,
Smell the wave of your passing fragrance,

Swim like April in the turn of your years,
See sweat form,
A perfect nipple,

On the surface of your smooth intemperate body.

A river of orange butterflies
Rushes through the woods,

A solitary goat is isolated on a hill,
A blue amulet swinging from the throat of an African child
Point to you,

The original brandy, the first fire.
Wrap around me in a whiskey kiss.
Awaken me with a science that has no name.

In shadows
I walk in you, follow you in wordless faith,
Winding,

A new unpredictable star,
Through nights
Of atypical celestial wandering.

I follow you, shimmering frog followed by a hungry fish,
Just below the water's edge,
With a ridge of teeth, phalanx of scales,

Cruising above the blind depths
Waiting for the oracle of your deep,
Your released coiled intoxicated hood

That captures and surrounds my head
Like a corps of five aroused
Supraluminous snakes.

Then you drop, inexplicably, below my eye-field
And I cannot see the stretch of your face
Moving from smile to awkward frowning,

Shifting, straining,
Trying to unfold like a hand
Caught in a tight nylon bag.

Without guidance, without light
Trailing you, the voice of a wounded dog
Lost somewhere in the dark,

Under the morning,
I head back to familiar ground, ground
Over the whirling peel of gravity the earth spools

Keeling on its way through the dark primordial waters
Existing long before the rise of our local sun…"
The first bird listened to his own voice listening to this,

Listened like a scabbard waiting for its blade,
Listened like a child's ear
For the echo of what always returns,

Listened for the rhetoric, for the laws of the wind
Woven through the herd of days
Where tooth and heart

Bind appetites for the body
The way our species nails the soul
With its carpentry of nerves

Into the sensuous noose of the eye,
The wet abyss of women, thighs. It was a prayer, a song,
Offering to a distant god,

Covered with metal, sitting in a dark room,
Refusing to come out. The walls felt it,
Cried out. The small stones felt it,

Tried to become smaller.
The crab's shell felt it
Quickened its molting

Under the glassy waters, the remote stars,
The reefs littered

With bits of cartilage and bone.

The first bird decided it was time to access
The best alibi of the world,
One with enough field force to fold

All the categories of color in the sky together
Proving in its passing the existence of worlds
Living beyond death, the rumors of the flesh.

This was the blue order,
The mythic encounter
With disowned dreams of our earlier fathers

Who crawled down from the trees,
Hid frightened in savannahs,
Pulled fire and speech from their throats.

For weeks nothing came of it.
He washed his brains with natron
In the divine lake but no fish came from its streams.

He tried psychiatric drugs
Mixed with talk, excoriations of the tongue.
Still the flag hung, listless, over the city of his body.

Finally he raised his head back up,
Up into the backyard of Orion's stars,
Calling down the shadowless Ones who long ago

Dissolved their own bodies
Into the folds of space
Where footpaths of the soul move through the enfolded orders.

A flutter of wings ricocheted
Off his beak, his oil slickened feathers.
The cage of reason collapsed in on him.

His hope, less than a grain of rice.
Everything he knew was vomited up,
Picked over garbage, leeches, the shells of eggs.

When emptied of suspicion,
Of money, of every image of vulvas and vaginas
Pulled deep from the interior of his Paleolithic heart,

He carried on through the newsreel
Of his days, lifetimes,
His flickering muscles, shifting new bodies,

The thick invention of his memory
On the plane he was on, *anything* he experienced as his.
Then he knew he was ready to start.

iv.

Return to the Blood

So how do we come to be;
The body crawling from an egg,
The swivel of bone, pillage

From the inward war of blood and salt?
Is it an oxcart of colors
From the mineral districts pulled into higher orders

Past the communions of orgasm and heat?
Is it the tiny blood-forms flowing
Where the loom of organs converge,

Gather their currents, carry them
To the growing
Outside the breakwater uterus?

Relatives across the earth suddenly arrive like great cows,
Ducks to the sudden scattering of crumbs

Feed in a barnyard.

They poke the navel; compare its eyes to a dead uncle
Or cousin or a weapon used
By lovers when it all ended badly.

In the summer of the body
There is a deep wine, a dark honey
Dreaming of returning to the bees,

Giving birth in the rioting clover.
There is an anarchist
During the night

Switching, rearranging the names for things
So that violence and beauty
Keep competing for the world.

There is a fragrant blasphemy
Mixing jasmine and orange
In a sacred discipline of oils

Presenting as libation
For the nose, the fingers, the ears.
There is a hidden alphabet,

A tonal sequence in soaring birds,
The rhythm of trees,
The immense ambition waters awaken,

Plunging over rocks and piers by the sea,
In the sound of cannon, dying women.
A renegade mammal wanders the marshes,

Hair delicate, brutal arms,
Eyes wide with music and brooding,
Filling us with metals, deadly force.

v.

The Passageway Up from the Skull

An orchard gate, broken,
Unhinged and open on a hill
Overlooks a stretch of field. The first bird,

Rising on a swell of morning,
Locks on the wind,
Feels the breath pulling through octaves

With the moving animals of the forest,
Hears the higher and lower pitches
Until his lungs are fully open.

The first bird takes on the skull of a man,
Newly dead, awakens from the mineral body,
Fumbles with language in a new key.

Then the stump of a tree: a womb-door opens.
Pirates swim in from the abyss.
Pulling sticks and weapons

From the shielded spaces under his wings
He calls into the red sky's hiss,
Rises on the accusatory hands of a clock.

It is the time of miracles,
The winter of forgiveness
When the scripture of memory mumbles,

Slides into mud-falls, washes away ashes
And the hair of sexually religious women
From the scenery of physically

Unrepentant men. The stump doubles into a spine;
The soul is caught in the wind,

Finds itself saddle-backed on a wild horse rising up,

Then pulled by the immense gravity of the sea
Toward a prophecy of salt mixing
With waves like propaganda

And released under a darker ambition of the sea.
Here the seed is most naked,
Stripped of everything except itself. *The spinal climb begins*.

Ripping off its wings the first bird
Takes on muscles, the pellucid eye of a snake.
The sainthood of a leopard

Is questioned, the veracity of a python,
The coral future of the hydra with its dumb
Exhausted heads tangled, swirling

Like a wounded octopus. Here
The red mouth of the soul
With its tail of lightning

Is sucked up the backbone
Into the brain's dark lines, its luminous fissures. Bird keeps on.
He bypasses the spinning cities,

Cuts through wheels, slices, like a Japanese sword,
Through the belly of his dreams opening like lily pads
Arranged in sequence over a watery path.

Each sang, or howled,
As he fell into the bottom of the swamp,
Then rose again,

Swan with a brutal nose, thorn of fire
Pointing toward the wingless secret
Tossed back and forth in the conversations of lighting and crows.

A smashed fly, dead, from backyard wars,
Lay on its side, wings blurred with excrement,
Eyes burnt-out, wide.

He thought of death,
The four noble truths once seen
Scrawled on the outside of a brown paper bag

Left crumbled at the feet of an itinerant drunk.
It was April, cherry blossoms had been
Fucking furiously with the bees

For months trying to come,
Trying to awaken the trees from their winterized sleep.
A Catholic church nearby was in flames;

A rabbi, nearly blind, was confused by his sudden attraction
To a young monk. Cherry tomatoes hung on vines
Like instruments of terror. Birds,

Stitched inside their own songs,
Flitted in and out of eternity.
A gray rag sank into the center of an elder man's eyes.

These were all promising signs. He was on
The right path. He could ignore the moon
With its white trenchant thrown at him

On nightly walks.
He could forgo eating at midnight,
Keeping his bowels clear for the morning;

His appetite locked up inside like vicious dog
Tamed, asking music with its meals,
Licking its balls when it wanted.

He kept his imagination from melting
Into the spoilage his mother warned him about.

He found his courage. He discovered

The marble base of identity
Fearing not even time or the erosion flowing
From an eroticized demon's breath.

He filled his soaring with an immense rush.
The caves, the ganglions, the veils gave way
To cities, boxcars and a fabulous oasis

Where singers of the mysteries convened
And luminous vocabularies were constantly invented by exotic,
    intoxicated women.
It did not distract him. He soared.

There were beautiful sounds leaking from space
Searching for purer ears to enter. He kept on. There were paintings
Great painters had meant to paint

Floating up from their skulls, long forgotten
Reverberations from their brightest days.
This did not distract him.

There was an eerie passageway
Rising up from his gut through the aorta
All the way to the root of his tongue

Bubbling out into his head
Like lava wrecking the shoreline of a terrified village,
Planting flags of cinders and light

Over the new earth. His *mentalized* world had evaporated.
The rational, the bone, the oblong and the mineral
Had fled. Even the black orchestra pit

The crows had reserved burned down
To charcoal, flicks of obsidian and gneiss. Curious beings
Slowing to the speed of light, peered into

The spinal river coursing his bloodlines, his organs,
The exhausted outline of his heart. Occupying his eyes,
They crawled inside him, looked out into his world,

Heard about from the Ones
Who had fallen, then returned, from the swamp of time and
    death.
Trees spoke their vernacular green.

Insects were the most organized.
Everything fed upon everything else
In a long chain with the meanest

Screeching at the others from the top.
So this was the bottom drawer of heaven
Where the underwear, the leftover bits of souls

Were dropped like discarded lemon rinds
Into a heap, buried with eggshells, seeds,
Obscene thoughts, the smell of rotting carnations.

Then the *alchemist beyond conception and form* fashioned a hand of
    light and salt,
Extended it down an elevator,
Then out an estuary, then through a seething tomb

Full of dead experiments,
Down into the uppermost head of the first bird.
Through a receding tunnel he could see it.

Beyond the chandeliers of light
He made out the form.
In the menagerie of his logic,

Under the covers of guilt, within the lust of the succubus
He could not quite renounce
He felt the icepick of sublime hammering

Trying to pry open his inner skull. Little explosions
Made it crack. Promises of celibacy
Sweetened the pot drawing up

His sexual fluids into the winding waterway of inner stars.
But this was a stopgap measure sure to fail
For the first bird loved to sing and fuck.

Then, then on the bold hypotenuse of his joy,
Grabbing filaments from the early flowers of creation,
He wrapped them round his pineal gland,

Pulled up with all the blackened nerves
Of his shimmering body
Until he could feel every boundary known

Collapse in the wake of a flailing star.
He thought what waits
In the emerging catastrophe of infinite autumn?

What reaches from the umbilical of stars
Into the centrifugal of every heart?
He settled down into the waters.

A trout looking upstream, current
Ululating, massaged him like hands
Over the robes of a medieval sultan's body.

      vi.

  The Ascent

There are legends in the salt, in the acid,
In the wine, trees
Dreaming of moving freely

In matter and light. In a museum numbers float by,
Ruined, along the road of history,

With darkened windows, piles of carpet, burned overcoats,

Lapels torn from the collars of corporate men surprised
By the sudden appearance of death
Dressed as a venomous spider

Slipping at night underneath the closet door. I understand this.
I leave these
To the fate of summer, to the calculation of apples

Falling with the accuracy of meteors and stars
Through the air, to autumn's widow
Moving her copper hands over the leaves, the hours.

The city is windy, the cocktail lounges boarded up;
Deserted malls fill with crows,
Burned mattresses, holes with rats, cellar doors broken off

From nearby houses, tossed
Into opened fields. I am tired of rattlesnakes
In the baby carriage, of past and future

Compressed into the symbols
My dreams inhabit. At times my fear becomes fire
As though I was the burning appetite

Of a small ambitious god materializing into a body. I will pull my
    intestines out,
Wrap them around trees like ancient Teutonic tribes
In celebration of the new Christmas in my mind.

Winds swallow me whole. The blue spider
Following every sadness
Attends to whatever I leave behind. On each side

Space within space opens before me.
A cruel vibrato in my brain
Spins out vertigo.

Then steadying my bones in the loom of flesh
I hold my liver, my fingers, my stomach in place,
Close my eyes,

Look upward to the right into the inner space I breathe,
Slowly twist my living self up and out
In a swoosh of fallen leaves

On a windy autumn day,
Rise, the beak of a phoenix from sleep,
Into the air beyond sleeping, dreaming or awake.

High windy planes are a sublime wine,
Harvest of minerals strengthening the bones
With sexual side effects of the moon

So full they spill out from the sky
Bathe souls pursuing them with the movement of embryos
Swimming, searching the subtle currents for an awakened uterus.

I came to the ambush of numbers,
Into the laurel surrounding the head
Of the strong, the indulgent,

The smooth and the lucent,
Ones moving over the prairies at night
In dreams of buffalo long departed their bodies,

Responding to the call of Apache,
Arapaho, names living in forgotten echoes,
In corridors of the red clay.

Numbers have dreamed me into these planetary swings
Around popular corners of the atom
Out into the wider spaces of nebulae, aurora,

Hidden elliptical languages of galaxies
Only seen recently

That we will not inhabit

Until our own bodies are vessels of light
Moving through the dimensions
Like salt through the foam.

vii

The Hour of the Blood

Everyman has a swastika in his heart,
Every woman an omen, an opal, a lance
Taken from the dark, wanting children

With an inborn knowledge of poetry and fire. Traveling upward
Through rivers of war,
The bones, holding the soul and appetites in place,

Braces like breakwaters against sea-waves of vision,
An orphanage of tongues, wall upon wall of
Burnt out ministries with airplanes,

Smoke, splintered organs of the young.
I have had a vision,
I have had a vision swim up the sea of my sleep

As I woke from the dream
Into the clearer sleep from which dreams and waking
Are but another dream.

In the wild waters of consciousness,
Fish and light-birds streaming
Past my eyes, I was pulled out to the space

Beyond the spaces of *insperience* and *experience*,
To the wider wave of stars, the inward sea,
Folding into each other in the warm neurocosmology

Of the earth. Pre-Ionian, pre-Egyptian,

Post-Lemurian before the Atlantian wars,
The old African of rivers warming my blood,

Moves along the shores of inward and outer life
Into the brain's core, the stellar places, seeding the worlds
Rising, drifting from Age to Age,

With new beings, races of light, emerged
From the deep core of infinite life.
Above my skull is opened.

Downward flowing angels, murals of death,
Transform the rising flight of a luminous bird
Undulating on wings,

With the black kiss of oblivion on his face,
Forever corrected and holding upright, ringing
As they pass back and forth

Beyond the blood-brain barrier into the labyrinth
Held up, strung on a floating latticework, a black nerve star,
Darker than the dark origin of matter and light.

The sibyls of physics have lied to us.
The laws of energy and death *not* everywhere
Equal, sometimes more passing in

Than out the sum of equations
Could possibly predict from one nodule of creation through the
    next.
Out this anonymous spasm of life

I pass, over the prairies of Enoch,
Over canyons with witches rising up,
Riding me through prisons of desire, hope,

Past the sanctuary where the robes and ropes
Are kept. I take wings rumored to hold

The dark deep laughter of god.

I pass through a tunnel of smoke,
The smile of dead cousins spread
On walls, doctoral degrees holding

Like antelope skulls, ambitions bleeding,
Insights colder than stones, aging organs on a tightrope of being,
    walking,
Leaning between one more stolen year and the next.

With only hours before the vessel finally leaves port
I move closer to the celestial rendezvous of angels and amoebae
Who cast lots for my body

Aeons before coming to this birth. Someday I will rush
Out my right hand and fist,
Up through the arm,

Then out the skull for the last time.
Taking the bird by its talons I'll
Hold on tight, fly through the squeeze

Of space between the spaces
Until all the breezes of earth are breeded out.
Over a lake with green traditions,

Heat turning into rocks, a being with blue arms
I will come to be, a cloud of disturbing color.
Gathering by the stones they will

Open their veins, let in the pure intuition of blood,
Pulsations of time, until it fills their fingers,
Then turn to me having forgotten

Every delusion of birth and death from a prior life,
Another home.
They will offer smoke, open the doors.

viii.

Bird Comes to the River of Beings

I searched the black river of your body
Looking for clues, rituals,
Things explaining the leaning of earth

Toward the center of spinning, the wider astronomy of birds
Swimming the air oblivious for weeks and aeons
Stretching before, after me, all

The spiraling dreams of my kind.
O master of the forms
And languages of the mouth

I set out daily moving, remembering the bottomless embrace of
     you
Folding over me in the night sky.
I wake each morning within a sheet of dreams,

Feel your luminosity receding from me,
A meteor
Escaping through space, trailing

The upper atmosphere, releasing forces in the wind
Science and melancholy fail to understand.
I have fallen through

Innumerable webs, traps
Set afloat, diving past the hand, the throat of beauty.
I have digested the strict particles of my world,

Seen them dissolve
In the blue quantum sea
Outside and beneath my eye.

I have ransomed my breath, tightened my body,

Dug holes in the belly of silence
To see a flickering of your presence

With a clear conscience,
A blameless appetite.
Constantly you are making overtures, music

I am incapable of hearing
Until I am completely still,
The sexual muses murmuring quietly

On distant hills,
Trees listening for over a thousand years.
O gatherer of waves and prodigies of the earth,

Reaper of the spinal songs,
The looms of the observant, the wise, the dark corridor visions of
    the blind;
O infinitely opening heart

Forgiving even Lucifer, Satan,
I come drifting between deaths,
Between oligarchies, parables of the flesh,

Theories of infinite regression toward some celestial mean
That keeps changing places
With waters, forms dancing in and out of emptiness.

Ocean beyond ego, synapse and molecular order,
Hidden personality in the microbe and stone,
I wear no watch,

Count the dead children flowing in the river under the mountains,
Fly over cities of fennel seed and grass.
In front of me my father dies

Lifetime after life

With beings passing back and forth honeycombing through your
    dark rift
In the heart of the Milky Way, handing me his shirt, his identity

I pass on
Marking the road for one form of us to flow into the next.
I fly on, riding gravity,

Bird wound in the blackness over meadows,
Children and associations littering
The earth below me.

Radiance is your predominant order,
Porcelain and starlight
The cells, the organs, the building blocks;

Each tissue of spacetime, every region of space,
Enfolding the others, mind unfolding them
In each form, occasion and act. And so

We come here
Dreaming differently from one life to the next
While still coming from another.

My hat tumbles down an empty road
Pockmarked with deserted houses,
Doors winging open

To the opulent air thick with birth, potency,
Fluent in all the animal powers.
I wish upon a collapsing star.

I fall inward into the great reef.
At the gate of astonishment thought withers away.
Autumnal leaves sucked into oblivion

By the final breath,
The feral cavity,

The octaves beneath the vibrating ear,

Filling what hears with a dissolving light
Outshining intuition, conception, and the last delusion of roses
Before they are gathered after the rains,

Thickening rooms with smell, oozing through our rib-bound
        bodies.
I fly within the *within* of things,
Swirling through the tunnel

With a white thorn of time
Pulsing between the seeding of worlds,
Emerge denuded of memory

With nurses, vases and waters coming down in hot baths,
Temple recollections, taxes,
Alphabets hanging and organizing minds,

Black oracular fascinations.
O compiler of evolutionary arcs
For the quark, the atom, the blood and the breath,

Take my hands,
Be my weapon against rigidity
Circumstance and the blue vaporous beings

Following me between deaths whispering
The vanishing anthems
And all that binds us to the body,

The bones, breath after breath,
Repeating the delusion we are stone and mucus,
Brain tissue at best within a bright collusion of circuitry,

Wishes holding out against
A vast being of meaninglessness and chance.
How strange, how beautiful

Being near you
Where electricity moves through curved spaces
And there is no rescue from gratitude or bliss.

        ix

Nameless

Noun and pronoun of a new body,
I am the devil's star, the finalized asterisk
Riding the wings of a risen snake.

More dense, more lucid,
More implacable and mutable than the wind,
More liquid and available

Than the oceans of the earth,
Capable of moisture, speech, forms without noise.
I am a traveler, a trader in jewelry and soap, moving between
    cities,

Between lights far to the north to centers
Buried in deep wells,
To caravans carrying desire across vast legends of land

Filled with horses, with children conscious
Of continually being reborn. I stretch out arms
Taken from rivers,

Mold music
Heard above savannahs, above grasslands swimming in winds
South of the azure mountains. I stretch my hands

Toward Emerald Tablets keeping
Vibratory the wisdom before the sphinx, before the pyramids,
Before the three buried paradoxes still unearthed.

I extend the blood beyond my veins,

Into air where I am born again and again,
A cloud of birds, dark forbidding swans

In a flume of white wings, long necks hooking their profiles
Around gravity, gathering stories
Of other worlds, storms,

Leaving behind tree trunks, limbs broken off,
Trailing dust of destroyed villages,
Nomads filling with an ominous disquiet.

I am a piece of coral
Bitten off by the sea, falling in slow motion
Toward bottom, soundless, bleached in the cinders of autumn.

x.

The Stone Turns

I am happiest when the surface of things washes over me,
Bringing me closer to essences, to hidden tides
Falling inward, not clinging to moorings

Habitually attached to movements under the moon's
Cold embrace.
I am the devil's star, a clockwork of misfortune,

A crow's explanation of death
Wrapped in the dense fabric of spacetime and events.
Whatever there is about flying over deep lakes,

African rituals, footprints stars leave
In the waters they pass over
On their way to more beautiful and imperishable things

I cannot even know.
My hands move as sea urchins,
Tentacles, fingers moving about, touching things,

Gambling on their forms, feeling them slowly
Draw up courage, assert the heart before
A drifting altar, watching them swimming their way

Back through fish and tides to the destination
Promised all life in carbon after the theater of death
Has washed everything away.

I remember almonds, brown girls,
Cities with vague agendas
Arguing their case before a supreme council

Where decisions are made and the verdict is always
More rain, more thunder, more elastic kisses
Carrying the guilty back further

Into flesh and time, Eve's dark adventure
Below the valley of the belly. The first bird,
A vast eye cruising the escarpment,

A campfire's lowering smoke, a horse
Abandoned by rider, tumbleweed cactus
The wind has played with, then abandoned

For the sound of running water quietly
Underneath a canyon no eye has ever seen.
The first bird is dreaming

Of an argument he had once with a small god.
Angels had been nervous for weeks;
Vipers and vulture capitalists

Were only beginning their work.
Vast networks in the netherworld
Of vibrating strings and quantum were ready to be yoked,

The design set, the architecture ready
For fingernail, asymptote.

It began well. God said *'let there be light,*

Hope, flawless perfection in the hills,
In icecaps, the mouth of moles. Let there
Be every kind of laughter and wisdom

Teeth can chew, move through strong muscles in the throat;
Let there be camels, microphones,
Gravity weaving matter together.

Let there be creatures dreaming themselves
Into the dim form of my own image
Strutting from planet to planet in ships of metal

Extracted from rare ores'. The angels applauded,
The first bird was silent. God saw this,
Then again spoke. 'Let there be religions for serpents,

Bifurcated atoms, trees waking up,
Walking about at night. Let there be oceans
Offering amendments quickly, without patents,

For luminous inventions of the five-finger folk;
Let minerals have a strange enduring mind'.
With yellow stones clenched between his feet

The first bird listened, took his time, spoke:
'There is already a river, a thick, luminous, opaque river
Running through manes of white foam

When the sea shakes exhausting itself
Against the bone of rocks
Holding fast as its thunder recedes.

There is a river, full of black fish, large and thoughtless,
Spooning in and out of shadows,
Blurring the edges between themselves

And steep oceans of dark matter. There is a river,
Currents stronger, quickening;
There are centuries of books

Holding echoes, crumbling landslides of shale
Sliding into bottomless waters,
Souls wandering between lifetimes and bodies

Waiting for a door
Back into the bloodstream and breath.
I make my nest here,

I strangle my children here,
I corner my choir here between the pews,
Smash the wood to kindling, burn songs and eyelids

Until the smoke builds up
Into a vortex dream sucking in the Caribbean,
The earth, the whole patchwork uterus of stars.

xi.

The Return of Desire

Lift me, a translucent fish, from celestial waters
And put me down among pines
Fallen sycamores

With great roots in bayous, headlands
Jutting out into the surrounding sea.
No form holds me more than an instant

Before bursting forth a new rabbit, a mole,
A fragment of cloth children toss
From playthings given and taken so many times

Fingerprints on them run like insects in swamps
Awakening for only a day in a decade then fading,

Leaving rumors of being begotten, forgotten,

Memories and templates
Of the life of the sea first emerging on to land.
They have come for something infinite in me

These hands, these gestures,
These signatures from moorings and mornings
Passing through me as I rewrite

The autobiography of my death.
Casting aside
The outlines of my body, pincushions and all, I threw away the
   blood,

The organs, the vestigial lungs sailing
From life to life, changing fingernails, molecules,
With the swiftness of a butterfly.

I came to the final desire, the final salt kiss
At the edge of the worlds
Where the names of god pass from memory

And there is only vibration,
The vast chamber of an ancient heart.
O how important people are always dying,

Their dogs and small flowers
Fed on by the shy, the temperate
Who make little sound, offend no one.

The beautiful, the ignorant are also dying,
Their souls in the crucible ground into detergent and pepper.
The world is always being constructed,

Torn apart again by great spiders. Approaching
The void with shoelaces and dreams,
The chamber opens, flies and diamonds escape,

And the sea falls down around it all,
Dense and wheeling
With a liquid cartography squid and octopus have loved

For a thousand thousand years before the first human had a name.
I walk, then fly, then flicker in and out of forms
Moving along the beach, my head open,

My eyes, caves mercenary birds veer through
With walls of obsidian and starlight,
Endless mirrors with stories of the pharaohs illegibly written on.

My tiny obscure vigilante soul,
A coil of indigenous fire
Metals and dark oils use to purify themselves.

Planets have given me my senses; from stars
With their guesswork, their celestial anatomy
I take the final moments of my births.

I wash myself in hours. I admit the limitation of teeth.
I love the alcohol made of lascivious berries from sacred trees
Whose roots river up

From the dark torque spooling with forces
At the center of the earth.
This is the hour, the republic, the winter

Seal bones wash on shore
Scattered among newspapers, bits of glass
Polished in the obsessive dialogue of the waves.

            xii

The New Birth

I once imagined the sea my mother
Full of overtones, bells,

Skyward-leaning musical adaptations,

Vibrations of the spleen, the liver, orchestral jazz
Pouring out of saxophone beings emerging in buttery sounds,
Taking up residence in the inner ear,

Reminding me not to be afraid of knowing
We really do not come from here
But from some entirely other place.

We are spies
With a curious fascination for wet kisses and death,
Addicted to Zen koans

We keep falling through.
O I imagined the sea my mother,
Her saxophone beings making buttery sounds

Visiting us curious, round
As a delicate planet
Whose trees release perfectly ripened fruit

With strange smells, intoxicants
Legal in all the contiguous states.
There is a saxophone with butternut color,

Sounds I have come to recognize
Among the wise and erudite
Living among us

Picking out patterns,
Listening quietly, equally, between those
Who feel beauty is a sacrifice

And those who believe nothing
Is more sublime than walking upright
Through the waters, collecting stones

Smoothed in the river of death.
Stick by stick, soul by soul
We keep constructing our local community in the universe.

Yarn from the weave of silk spiders,
Colors from swans
On a thousand-year quest,

Are molded, exquisitely hand by hand,
Into fabric thinner than an eyelash,
Strung across the chest,

Whispering in words of an ancient covenant. Erudite owls,
The mumbling stutter of bees,
The sacrifice of forces at the center of the atom

Are balanced, held forth, finally compared
With their own resonance
Until the secret name of their passion is rounded and understood.

All mothers bear the sea within them,
Awaken the sea within us,
Bring us to this place;

An inverse square image of ourselves projected
From a dimension of light,
Sibling to photons, but more subtle,

Not made crude by birth or death.
The saxophone, between brassy silences,
Smoky undertones,

Has this resonance it shares with the sea,
The birthing place,
The engines pulling worlds into breath.

We walk with hands crossed,
One finger free, pointing

Toward the signal always

On the other side of the swamp.
Each footstep is a tax on beauty
Reaffirming the heartbeat

Marking our passing across the void
Into the purer ellipse where the deathless await
Our long-anticipated arrival.

                xiii

Return to the Body

Original dust return to me,
Embrace me, a rising flower in the hurricanes
Tossed this way and that, looking for summer

In the long stretches of grass
Between the shoreline
And the dark city with its shadowy, benevolent birds.

I am pulled into the purple afterglow of the beach
Where the wind has entered a wild marriage
With sunlight and the death of the world

Pours down its red into the twilight.
Some ambitious stage manager
From a forgotten landscape

Has tried again and again
To remember
The final voice of god.

As it lingers in the ear as I drift further and further out to sea.
Conch shells enfold a primordial rhythm.
A seagull lifts an ancient wing.

Parties of ominous clouds hurl over the horizon

Promising to meet the morning
With thunder, with the sound of bestial mermen

Assaulting the beach.
This alienation from light,
This estrangement from infinity

I feel as the dolphin feels gazing into the midnight sky
At the Dog Star watching the celestial equator.
The hot temper, the breath of the newly dead

Passes in a cold wind;
The echo of sea animals stranded on land,
The waves failing to reach them

Even with the moon at its peak.
I emerge, fiery dream of an opaque bird,
Rise toward astonishment,

Dissolve at the moment of realization,
Fall back to earth in a shimmering sheet of illusions, images
Innumerable lives reflected

In billions of fables of the fall, the rediscovery of man.
I have made this journey
Clasping the hands of an itinerant sailor

Long left the world of flesh, of teeth,
For the border of music and insight
Where rain pauses,

Becomes the tiny cold white fruit winter makes,
Scattered in the ruins of the heart.
I obey markers found

In eyes of the beautiful, the loquacious;
Trust moving parts the blind feel.
Time, an oasis for beings of light

Who come here, visiting,
From spaces with no limit on all pervasive consciousness.
Battling this beautiful disease,

Falling into corruptible books,
I attend to signs, symbols of an unearthly economy.
The ambient sea is angry and immense.

About the Author

    Edward Bruce Bynum is the author of several books of poetry and the winner of the national Naomi Long Madgett Poetry Prize for *Chronicles of the Pig & Other Delusions*. He is a clinical psychologist, author of several books in psychology, including *The Dreamlife of Families, DARK LIGHT CONSCIOUSNESS* and *The Roots of Transcendence*. He is a recipient of the Abraham H. Maslow award from the American Psychological Association. He lives in the Amherst Massachusetts area.